Make Money Photographing Corporate Headshots

How I Make Over $100,000 a Year

Bradley Lau

©2020 Bradley Lau

All rights reserved. No portion of this book may be reproduced in any form without permission from the publisher, except as permitted by U.S. copyright law. For permission contact:

Brad@BradleyLau.com

www.BradleyLau.com

All product names, logos, and brands are property of their respective owners. All company, product and service names used in this book are for identification purposes only. Use of these names, logos, and brands does not imply endorsement.

Table of Contents

About Bradley Lau 1
Introduction 2
Chapter 1: Equipment Needed... 3
Chapter 2: Camera Settings & The Battle for Light 6
Chapter 3: Lighting Settings... 12
Chapter 4: Client Locations & Home Studios....................... 14
Chapter 5: Position of Subject & Background....................... 17
Chapter 6: Lighting & Positioning... 19
Chapter 7: Shooting Tethered.. 22
Chapter 8: Photo Composition.. 24
Chapter 9: Building Rapport with Your Subject.................... 25
Chapter 10: Posing the Subject 28
Chapter 11: Common Subject Problems............................... 32
Chapter 12: Reviewing the Shoot... 38
Chapter 13: Retouch & Delivery.. 39
Chapter 14: Your Company Details...................................... 41
Chapter 15: Website & Domain Names................................ 43
Chapter 16: Your Portfolio... 45
Chapter 17: The Answer is Yes!... 47
Chapter 18: Marketing 48
Chapter 19: Invoicing... 52
Chapter 20: Pricing... 53
Chapter 21: Miscellaneous Best Business Practices 55
Chapter 22: Final Thoughts 57
Chapter 23: Resources.. 58

About Bradley Lau

I'm just a regular guy who probably knows technically less than most photographers out there. I never went to school for photography and never dug into the technical details. Despite this I make well over $100,000 USD a year as a professional headshot photographer, with nothing given to me and no established connections. I continue to make mistakes and could probably double what I make if I took all the advice that I'm giving to you here in this book. But what I do have is longevity, interpersonal skills and a desire to make my clients happy. I've been at this for 17 years and will attempt to teach you what I know.

Introduction

As a photographer with almost 2 decades experience, I have shot many genres including (Real Estate, Weddings, Family Portraits, Products, Bar Mitzvahs, Parties, Corporate Events, & Pets). I first started shooting Actor Headshots and now after all these years, I only shoot Corporate Headshots.

I will attempt to teach you everything you need to know but will also attempt to be as brief as possible. I'm not going to teach every aspect about photography, but I am trying to get you started as fast as you can. If you pursue photography, it will be a never-ending journey of learning and experimentation.

This book is written for a complete beginner. But if you are an experienced photographer, you can skip the parts you know. I know you will find some valuable information here that will help you with your headshot business.

Also keep in mind that every photographer has a different style and way of shooting. There is no one right or wrong way of doing things. I'm going to show you what works for me and what I do. Don't ever think that you have to copy someone exactly. Just take what you like from each photographer, as you learn to develop your own style and way of doing things.

As I said, I make well over 100K a year for the past few years, shooting **only** Corporate Headshots. Your market may or may not support this. You can certainly shoot performer headshots to add to your income as well as other genres.

Keep in mind, success will take time. Do not be overwhelmed. As the saying goes, "How do you eat an elephant? One bite at a time."

The longer you are in business, the more money you will make. Add new clients each year and your phone will keep on ringing every day. But you certainly don't have to wait 17 years for success.

Chapter 1: Equipment Needed

If you are starting from scratch, you will need at a bare minimum, about $2,000 worth of gear, plus a decent computer. You can put this on a credit card and hopefully make it back quite quickly. If you are crackhead broke and can't afford this, then this isn't for you. If you already have everything that you need, even better!

You basically need a camera, a lens, 3 lights, 3 light modifiers, 3 light stands and a reflector with stand. Having said that, I did a shoot recently outside with only one speedlight and one umbrella.

Camera

You can use a **DSLR** body or the newer technology **mirrorless** camera body. These will come either as full frame or crop sensor. The **full-frame** bodies have larger sensors and cost more. **Crop-sensor** bodies have smaller sensors and are cheaper. In addition, crop sensor bodies have a 1.5x or 1.6x multiplier on the focal length. This means if you put a 50mm lens on a crop sensor body, it will be the equivalent to a 75mm or 80mm on a full frame body. In the end, it doesn't matter what you start with, buy what you can afford. The rule seems to be, spend your money on good glass.

Lens

For headshots, I would suggest any lens between 85mm and 200mm, but nothing wider (smaller) than 85mm for full frame cameras. If you have small backgrounds, shoot at 200mm as it will compress the background and make it look bigger and closer.

On a crop sensor, you can figure between a 50mm and 130mm.

Faster lenses, those with large aperture openings of f/2.8 and lower, allow more light, create creamier blurred backgrounds and naturally are more expensive than a typical kit lens.

Accessories

Memory cards store your images. Buy a decent brand like SanDisk, 64GB and up. Don't skimp on bargain brands here. You don't want to lose your images. Format your cards in camera before each shoot. Make sure the existing files have been uploaded.

Make sure you have an extra camera **battery** and keep it charged.

Types of Lights

There are **LED** lights that you plug in and are constant, so you can see the light on your subject.

There are studio **strobes** which also plug in and can contain a lot of power. They go off only when you press the camera shutter, but they usually have **modeling lights** you can turn on to give you an idea of how the light will look and its direction.

Speedlights are small battery powered flashes that are versatile, but not as powerful as strobes. The Godox brand AD200's (currently popular) are a slightly larger, more powerful speedlight. You can't see the light until the you press the shutter.

There are also **Compact Florescent** bulbs that are used mostly by amateurs, but they still work.

Light Diffusers

In general, the larger the diffuser, the softer the light. Soft light creates a nicer look with softer shadows. Get the biggest light modifiers you feel comfortable with. Keep in mind, your space may not allow for very large modifiers.

Umbrellas are a simple way of diffusing the light. They are the easiest to setup.

Softboxes are a bit more complex and sometimes control the spread of the light better. They are shaped as squares or rectangles.

I use 39" deep umbrellas. I like the convenience of them. With added diffusion panels, they act like softboxes.

Light Stands

Come in varying heights and weights. I buy light stands based upon the size of my bag. I like lightweight, compact ones, but they can fall over easily if knocked into. It is not that important what kind you get.

Computer

I will assume you have a computer already. Whatever you have will work. I personally work on a MacBook Pro, but use what you have.

Tripod

I'm not a fan of using a tripod for headshots. One more thing to carry and it feels a bit restrictive. I will say though, if you are using a 70-200mm lens, you may consider it as its heavy and more prone to motion blur.

Chapter 2: Camera Settings & The Battle for Light

It is imperative that you know how to use all of your camera settings. Get your camera manual out and read it cover to cover. Do research online to see what each feature does. For simplicity, I will only go over the most important settings that you need to control.

At the end of the day, photography is all about light and controlling it. We either have too much or not enough. An over exposed image has too much light. An underexposed image does not have enough. We have a number of settings at our disposal to increase or decrease the amount of light that is needed to create the perfectly exposed image.

The Exposure Triangle: The Basics of Manual Mode

The exposure triangle consists of three things: **ISO, Aperture, and Shutter Speed**. Always remember, there is a price to pay for using each of these settings. Keep this in mind. There is never a one-off solution for getting more light as the price you have to pay for one setting may be too much. In other words, each setting has its downside.

ISO

For the most part, I keep this the same for all of my shoots and rarely change it. ISO determines how "sensitive" the image sensor is to light. A lower number 50 or 100 will produce a darker image. So why wouldn't you always use a higher ISO if you needed more light? Well the price to pay is higher noise. The photo will be grainy at a higher ISO. Crisper images will always be shot with a lower ISO. **I usually set my ISO to 160** which is quite low. When you spend more money on a camera body, one of the features is its "low light sensitivity". This basically means you can shoot at a higher ISO without producing as much noise. You can however remove a lot of the noise in post-production with Adobe Lightroom™ or Photoshop™.

Aperture (f/stop)

This pertains to the size of the opening in the lens. The smaller the number, the larger the opening, hence the amount of light that enters the camera. An aperture of f/1.8 allows more light in than let's say f/8. F/22 will not let in much light at all. A lens that has a low number aperture, let's say f/1.4 is considered to be a "faster" lens than one with a minimum aperture of f/4 and is usually more expensive. In a darker environment, you would usually use a low number aperture. But as I said, there is a price to pay, which for aperture is depth of field.

Depth of Field refers to the closest and farthest objects in an image that are in focus. If you take a headshot with an aperture of f/1.8, when you focus on the eyes, the ears may be out of focus. This shallow depth of field setting of f/1.8 would allow a lot of light in but would be bad for let's say a group shot with multiple rows of people. The people in the back row would be blurry if you focused on the front row.

If you want a blurry background, you would shoot with a low number f/stop (1.4, 1.8, 2.8, 3.2)

"Bokeh" is a term that refers to the quality of this background blur.

I usually shoot headshots with an f/stop of f/3.5 or f/4.0

If the background is a solid color like white or black, the blur is never an issue. But if you are using the client's office or window as a background, you will want the blur.

Shutter Speed

This is the amount of time the camera shutter is open. A slow shutter speed allows more light to enter the camera. It is usually a fraction of a second. **I usually shoot with a shutter speed of 160.** This is actually 1/160th of a second.

A shutter speed of 80 would be slower and would allow more light into the camera. Its open for 1/80th of a second. It's basically open twice the amount of time and will allow that much more light in.

So, if you need more light, you could hypothetically shoot at 20 which would be 1/20th of a second, but what is the price to pay? With a slow shutter speed, if you hand hold a camera, you will get camera shake and therefore your photos will be blurry. Or your subject will move a bit and the image will be blurry. So you would never really shoot at 1/20, especially handheld.

There is a general rule which states that your shutter speed should never be slower than your lens focal length. This applies when you are hand holding a camera and the subject can move. So, if you are shooting with a lens that has focal length of 85mm, you should shoot at 1/85 or faster like 1/100, or 1/160 which is where I generally shoot.

Also keep in mind, you can usually not go faster than 1/200 of a second if you are using strobe flashes or speedlights (for Canon). If you ever see a photo with a black edge, this is the reason; your shutter is too fast.

There is a way around this called High Speed Sync, which you can read about in your flash's manual. With High Speed Sync on, you can increase the speed of your shutter (less light). Shutter speed controls the available or ambient light. I rarely use this.

So that's the exposure triangle. In summary, I usually shoot 160 ISO, 160 shutter speed (1/160th) and an f/stop of f/4.0.

White Balance

Every type of light has a color to it. I'm sure you've seen photos that looked too warm (yellow) or too cool (blue).

Light color is measured on the **Kelvin Scale**.

Shade 7000 (Blue)
Cloudy 6000
Strobe 5500
Daylight 5200
Florescent 4000
Tungsten 3200 (Yellow)

When you are in a room, you may have window light which is one color, overhead lights which may be another color or a mix of colors if its mixed lighting, and then the color of the lights that you are using.

You need to tell the camera what kind of light you are using. I manually dial in the Kelvin number which tends to be around 5500.

Don't use Auto White Balance as you will see that each picture you take, may change color slightly.

File Type

There are two basic file types, JPEG or RAW. RAW files are much larger and contain more information and give you more flexibility when you go into post processing. For instance, if you overexpose an image, it is easier to fix a RAW photo than it is to fix a JPEG. But most people can't view RAW images and they need to be processed. JPEG files are essentially already processed by the camera itself.

I shoot RAW and then retouch them and convert to JPEG for my clients. My current camera, the **Canon 5D Mark IV**, gives me a choice for Medium RAW (27.7MB) which are slightly smaller files and I use this setting. Regular RAW images (36.8MB) are just too big for me and take more disk space and are slower to download. I will use standard RAW if I know the client wants to make large prints of the photos. When I shoot photobooth type events where I am taking hundreds of headshots and delivering them instantly via email without retouching, I use S2 JPEG (1.3MB).

Keep in mind all of the settings that I use are just a guideline to start with. As different situations arise, these settings are adjusted.

My Camera Settings Summary:

ISO: 160
f/stop: 4.0
Shutter Speed: 160
White Balance: K setting \Manually set around 5000-5500
File Type: Medium RAW

Always check your settings. Make sure all of your camera and light settings are properly set. It's easy for something to change, a button moved, etc. and it can have a major impact on your shoot. Run through each setting before you start and a few minutes into the shoot.

In the past I have had:

- Auto Focus switched off and I didn't realize it. I'll sometimes turn the auto focus off to take a quick photo when I am testing the tether connection. I forgot to turn it back on, but the photos still looked good, but they weren't tack sharp.

- Aperture dial not locked and I accidently changed the f/ stop and thus the exposure. My camera has a lock button so this doesn't happen, but sometimes I don't use it.

- Image Stabilizer on lens not set correctly. It should be ON when hand holding and OFF when camera is on a tripod.

- Flash units off, set to wrong group, or dead batteries.

- White balance custom set to the prior shoot.

- File size not updated from prior shoot. (99% of time I shoot with Medium Raw. I occasionally change to Small JPEG; not switching back can be a disaster.)

The moral of the story is to go slow, be methodical and most importantly, be aware of how your images look. You've got the benefits of digital, so use them. The old film days, we didn't have this luxury.

Chapter 3: Lighting Settings

This is going to be different for each type of lighting equipment, so this will only work if you use similar lighting to mine. I use speedlights, the portable camera flashes that are popular. They are small and run on rechargeable AA batteries. I like them for their portability and lack of wires that can be tripped over. They offer plenty of power for headshot photography.

If you already have lights, then use what you have. There is no right or wrong system or way of doing things. Continuous LED lights are also nice if you have them. Powered studio strobes offer a lot more power and are also fine. Because I am always traveling to client locations by foot, subway or cab, I wanted the most portable setup as possible. If you are shooting out of your home or studio, or if you have a car that you will drive up to your clients parking lot, portability isn't as important.

I usually set all my speedlights to maximum of 1/8 power. 1/1 would be full power. So basically 1/8 power is using only 12.5% of the speedlights output. I do this so I don't overwhelm the batteries and it gives them a faster recycle time. In other words, I don't have to wait so long in between shots. If you shoot too fast, the second shot will be darker as the flash won't have a chance to fully charge.

Not every light will be on the same power. We will discuss in more detail later.

Each light is also assigned a letter A, B and C where I can control each lights power separately.

As with your camera, familiarize yourself with the speedlight manual or whatever lighting manual you have.

Speedlight Transmitter Settings

I control my individual speedlights with a radio transmitter (Canon ST-E3E-RT) that I attach to the top of my camera.

Set the mode to M (Manual), set the ratio to ABC
Press GR to Group A and change the Key light's power to 1/8
Press GR to Group **B** change the **B**ackground light's power 1/16
Press GR to Group C and change the hair light's power 1/16

These are approximate numbers and will change from shoot to shoot. For instance, blonde and gray hair don't require as much light as dark black hair. Also, dark skinned clients require more light.

Chapter 4: Client Locations & Home Studios

I currently do not have a photo studio and spend 90% of the time shooting in corporate conference rooms. Some are tiny, some are large. The other 10% of the time, I shoot in my Manhattan living room which is small. It's never perfect and I would love to have more space, but you **use what you got**. It doesn't make sense for my business to rent a photo studio. It would be like $3,000 a month even for something tiny. Manhattan is great for some things, but cheap rent isn't one of them. Every once in a while, I will find space that I can rent by the hour if my client doesn't want to use their space for whatever reason and they have multiple people coming. I'd rather not have a group of people come to my home. Search online for office space by the hour. Reach out to local photo studio owners. They may be happy to get some extra income. Breather.com is a website that lists hourly commercial space for use in Boston, DC, Chicago, NY, LA, London, Montreal and Toronto. There may be something similar in your area. They are my go to choice when I need space. I can get room for $50 per hour.

If you are shooting corporate headshots, more than likely, you will be going to your client's office, usually setting up in a conference room. I NEVER move tables and only move chairs on one side of the room. If its big enough, I won't move anything. If there is a window in the room, try and setup so you as the photographer have your back to the window. This will allow for the subject's pupils to close so more of the colored iris will be visible. Be aware of any overhead lights that may mess up your lighting. Put something down on the table so you don't scratch it with any of your gear. Bring a handheld mirror. Mark a spot on the floor with tape to designate where the subject will stand. I use 2" blue painters tape. Use a good brand like 3M as off brands are sometimes useless and don't stick to carpet. Gaffers tape is also good but sometimes is difficult and can mark certain surfaces.

I always ask clients for the biggest room that they can spare, and it doesn't need windows, but I'll work with whatever you give me. At times, I had to setup so that I was shooting outside of the doorway to give myself some extra distance. Adapt and adjust; two words to live by.

Remember when you leave to neaten up the room. Put everything that you've moved into its original position. Try and leave it neater than when you arrived. Always do a lap around the room checking to see if you forgot to pack up any equipment. I have in the past left a battery and charger in the wall and had to go back to retrieve it. I now have a sticker with my company info on it in the event it happens again.

Get a list of everyone's name for the shoot, the time they are to appear and their phone numbers. That way if they are late you can call them. One person late can have a domino effect on the rest of the people scheduled.

Home Studio

I always think about my client's comfort. Make it easy for them to get to your studio. Don't have them walk forever deep into your basement where they may be wondering if they are about to be murdered. I would recommend a space they can see as soon as they enter and not have to wander through multiple rooms viewing your personal belongings.

Keep the space super bright and as uncluttered as possible. It should smell fresh as well. Paint the walls white if you can. Colored walls may produce color cast.

Have a coat rack separate from your own clothes. I use one of those racks you hang over the door. Hang up your client's clothes with nice hangers. Sometimes people will have their shirts or jackets in a bag. Hang them up immediately so they don't wrinkle. While you could provide an iron and board, I tell my clients to bring clothes freshly pressed on hangers. But you would be surprised how many people roll their clothes into a ball and stuff them in a bag.

Have a large mirror in a well-lit area where they will be standing. Some photographers like to have their subjects sit. I did that with actor headshots when I shot them years ago, but with corporate, I prefer they stand. They can have better posture and suit jackets don't buckle up as much.

Offer them bottled water or a coffee if you have everything to make a quick cup. Present it nicely. You are building rapport and are trying to make your subject feel at ease. Create a separate drink station for your clients. Don't walk away into the kitchen if its far. Have a nice tray and small table for the beverages, lint roller, etc.

Make sure the temperature is comfortable. People are sometimes late and are rushing and maybe sweating a bit. I crank up the air conditioning before they arrive on hot days. You don't want extra shiny, sweaty subjects.

Subjects will often ask to use your bathroom. Make sure it is decluttered and clean as well. And check the bathroom before your client leaves. Often, they will leave something there by accident. You don't want your wife asking, "whose bra is this?"

As the old saying goes, first impressions count. You don't want your client to form any negative opinions of you before the session even starts.

Your desk should be clean and clutter free. Make sure your computer screen is clean as well. I use alcohol wipes to clean the screen when it is off to see the grime.

Have cleaning wipes, hand sanitizer and anything else you can think of to make your clients feel comfortable.

Chapter 5: Position of Subject & Background

Try and keep your subject at least 5 feet away from the background to avoid shadows showing up on the background. The more space the better.

Backgrounds

I always stress to beginners that the background of a photo is just as important as the subject. This is my number one piece of photography advice to all beginners.

The background may be lit or unlit depending upon the look you are going for.

A round gradient at shoulder level is a common look. Use a light with a grid attachment to create this effect. I recommend this look. You can also place the light to one side of your subject as well.

A gray background may look white if you blast enough light on it.

A gray background may look black if you have no light on it and the subject is far enough away from it and no light from the key, fill or rim are spilling on to it.

If you are trying to get the background to look perfectly white, be careful to make sure that light is not reflecting back and spilling on to you subject. Take a picture and zoom into their hair and shoulders. They should not look "cloudy" but have strong contrast against the background. If it does look cloudy, move the subject further away from the background. If you don't have the space, then lower the light settings. While not always ideal, you can always make the background white in post-production.

Also, the further your subject is from the background, the more blurred out it will be which is often a pleasing look. But if you are shooting against a solid color, then distance is not that important.

Window as a Background

A blurred window as a background with the cityscape makes for a great background for a headshot.

But shining lights on a window makes highlights. Try and angle your camera so that you are not shooting directly at the window, but at an angle to it. Definitely allow yourself more time to setup. You may need to move the lights further away from the sides of the window, so they are not reflected in it. I always take a photo of the window background, focusing at the same distance I would if the subject was there, WITHOUT flashes. I can then use this as a master for other shoots or use it to help with retouching.

As previously stated, I recommend shooting between 85mm-200mm. If you shoot at 200mm, the actual size of the background will not have to be as big as it brings it closer and enlarges it in the photo. Naturally you will also have to stand further away. By shooting at 200mm, the background will be even blurrier than if you shoot at 85mm.

See https://shootforthemoney.com/headshot-book/ for an example photo of 85mm vs 200mm

The most common corporate backgrounds are gray or white. Black can also look good if the lighting (Hair\Rim\Background) is correct. I use mostly collapsible backgrounds that are easy to prop up and travel with. I also use seamless paper but its harder to travel with. Since I just shoot headshots, I use the smaller 53" rolls and not the longer 107".

Chapter 6: Lighting & Positioning

Lighting Terms

Key Light – This is your main light that will do most of the lighting.

Fill Light - As the name suggests, this light is used to "fill in" shadows and will usually not be as powerful as the key light. Instead of a fill light, you can also use a reflector.

Rim Light\Hair Light\Kicker – This light is used to separate the subject from the background. It will create an edge of highlights and will add contrast to an image. There may be more than one.

Background Light – As the name suggests, will light the background.

General Lighting Basics

1. Put the light higher than their face by about a 2 feet pointing down.

Humans are used to light coming from above in the form of the sun or overhead lighting. This is why when you were a kid and someone put a flashlight below their chin and lit their face, they looked scary or not quite right.

2. Point the light so it doesn't directly hit their face, but just misses in front of them. This is called "feathering" the light.

3. Soft light is ideal. You don't want harsh shadows. When a light source is closer to the subject, it will produce softer shadows. Bring the light as close to the subject as you can. The larger the light source, the softer the light, so closer is better. Your lights may end up in the photo and you will have to retouch them out. This is easy for solid backgrounds, but more work for windows and office environments. Try and crop the lights out of the image.

4. Light modifiers are used to soften and shape light. An umbrella is the simplest to setup and use. By pointing the light into the umbrella, it will spread out and bounce back larger. But umbrellas tend to "spill" more light as they are not as directional as softboxes. They basically do the same job, but come in a variety of shapes and sizes, usually square or rectangle. The shape of the catchlight, the reflection in the eye is based on the shape of the light modifier. Catchlights give sparkle to the eyes and you can get some hints as to what kind of lighting is used when you zoom into the eyes of a photo.

You can sometimes bounce the light off of a white wall or ceiling to create a giant softbox.

5. Flat light is not ideal. Flat light comes when the light source is placed directly in front of the subject. If you attach your flash directly on the camera, it will come in front and be too flat and even. There will be no highlights and shadows which usually make for a nice image. By placing our lights on stands, the light becomes "directional" and by using "light modifiers" like umbrellas, we shape and soften the light.

Use a piece of tape on the floor where you want your subject to stand or sit.

Place the **Key light**, the main light at a 40-45-degree angle about two feet from them with the light just feathering past their face. I usually stand on the tape, where the subject will be, so I can see and adjust the position of the light.

The **Fill Light** can either be directly behind you the photographer, or slightly to the right of you. It shouldn't be as powerful as the key light. Its purpose is to fill in the shadows. The fill light should also be high and pointed down and should dissect the key light. Imagine the key light and fill light shoot laser beams and they should cross directly in front of the face of the subject, an inch in front of their nose.

As an alternative to a fill light, I now use a **silver reflector** that is positioned directly in front of the subject, horizontal to the floor at waist level or higher. It will reflect the light from both the key and hair lights into the subject's face and neck. Position it as close to the subject's face as you can without having it in the photo.

Hair Light is usually placed behind and off to the side of the subject. It is usually positioned directly opposite the key light. Make sure the light does not shine into the camera lens. This is an important light, as it will help create separation from the background and will add dimension to the photo. Don't skip using this light, as it really makes a difference and makes the images more professional looking.

Background Light is usually placed 2-3 feet in front of the background, placed low enough so that the subjects body hides the light and its stand from the camera. This position will change if you are using the office environment as the background. You will have to experiment.

See https://shootforthemoney.com/headshot-book/ for lighting setup ideas.

Chapter 7: Shooting Tethered

I personally like to shoot tethered to a laptop, so that each photo I take gets sent from my camera to my laptop and can be viewed instantly. It's a great way to give feedback to your client so they can see what they are doing or how they look. They may for instance think that they are smiling big, but when you show them the shot, they can see that they are not. Or they may want to try a certain hairstyle. I'm always open to trying new things, but there is a short amount of time so a quick test can determine the right path to take.

I use Adobe Lightroom Classic™ to tether my camera. Other photographers use Capture One™.

I use a tether cable to connect to my camera to my computer. I have a 15' orange cable from Tether Tools. They are expensive, but they are considered the go to brand. You can tether wirelessly, but this can be slow.

Using the Adobe Lightroom Classic™ menu:

File\Tethered Capture

Start Tethered Capture

Session Name: ##_##_##_CompanyName (I use the date and the company name)

Check off Segment Photos by Shots (This creates a subfolder for each person's name when you are photographing multiple people)

Naming Template: Session Name - Sequence (This will create a longer file name)

Destination: I only choose this one time. I usually make a folder for each year. I call mine 2020Headshots in the Pictures folder (Mac)

When a new person comes in, I press SHIFT\COMMAND T on my Mac and type in the next person's name. This will create a new folder.

Show a few shots, but don't let the subject view the laptop during the shoot. If they can see each shot, they will spend all their time focusing on the laptop and not on you and your direction. It becomes a distraction and the flow of the shoot will be ruined.

Not Shooting Tethered

This will certainly speed things up for you. No technical issues to deal with and no review time spent with the client or clients. You will just upload the photos for the client to see after the shoot. This certainly has its benefits.

You can still show the client the photos on the back of the camera, so they have an idea of how they look, but you can't end session knowing what files need to be retouched.

You then have added work to upload afterwards and wait for the client to pick their favorites. Decide what works for you.

Chapter 8: Photo Composition

It is important that you speak with your client to get an understanding of what they want. While your style may be different, you will often need to match what they already have. Most of the time, corporate headshots go on a company website and they want to have a uniform look. Some clients want the full shoulders in the shot, while some want tight crops. Some want waist up, but that is rare. Some want you to shoot horizontally, while most want vertical.

My suggestion is for you to shoot horizontally so both shoulders are fully in the photo and then shoot down to the elbow. This gives you enough room to crop in any way.

Important tip: Shoot with enough room on top of their heads so that if they crop the photo in circle, there will be enough background in the photo for them to effectively to do so.

I personally prefer to crop with only an inch of space is above their head and cut both shoulders out down to their armpits. It's a standard crop for me. Look at your clients' website or other company websites to see how they crop their photos.

Many companies will have a printed set of guidelines for the photographer to follow.

In the end, it's always best to have more, as you can always crop out what you don't want. More dead space above the head, more body showing, perhaps to the elbow.

Group Shots

If you shoot a group shot for your clients, make sure the spacing is consistent between each person. It's a common complaint when the gaps are different for each person.

Chapter 9: Building Rapport with Your Subject

This is probably the most important aspect of your photoshoot. When shooting **corporate headshots**, most of your subjects will tell you they hate getting their photo taken and are not happy that they have to get it done. That negative attitude will certainly have an effect on the outcome of the session. It's super important to put them at ease. I do this by having a quick chat with them before and during the session. Just knowing what they are getting into will put them at ease. I'll first explain exactly what the process is.

"Hello X, it's nice to meet you. My name is Brad and I promise I'll do my best to make this as quick and painless for you as possible. So, here is what's going to happen. I'll take about 30 shots, we will look at them together, and then you will pick your favorite photo. That favorite will then get retouched so you will look even better than you already do. Don't worry, we won't change you, but just give you a nice spa treatment. A little smoother skin, an extra hour sleep under your eyes, get rid of any stray hairs, shine, lint, etc."

They will often always make some positive comment about retouching. Play along with them. "Oh, can you take all my wrinkles away?"

"You want me to make you look 20 again?

I'll continue to say:

"There are 3 important things to remember.

1st, look dead center into my camera lens, look inside it, don't just look "at" the camera.

2nd, when I ask you to move, I only want you to move an 1/8 of an inch. I'll always be a mirror image, so you'll know what direction I want you to move in. I'll always guide you, so you don't have to worry about how to pose. I may ask you to "turtle", that is bring your nose and face forward, without leaning your body and then I'll demonstrate, joking that this was one of my 80's dance moves. This will strengthen the jaw line.

And lastly, we want you to look confident and approachable. Confidence comes from great posture so think of a hook and rope attached to the top of your head pulling your spine thru the ceiling.

Most importantly, approachability comes from your smile. So, for the smiling photos, do not smile for the camera. It will look forced and fake. I want you to think about something that you have an emotional connection to that makes you happy.

Think about something or someone you love. If you weren't at work, what you like to be doing and who would you like to be doing it with? And for the next few minutes, your thoughts don't have to be legal or moral, if it helps you to get a great smile."

If they are struggling during the shoot, I'll ask if they are a fan of any sports teams. If they are, I might suggest they imagine themselves scoring the winning point of the next championship or celebrating in the locker room. You have to read your subject. Make the interaction as fun and as enjoyable as you can.

During the session, I'll also ask where they were born and see if I can make any connections. I'm a big hockey fan, and often include that in my rapport building. It doesn't matter if they are, but they then may tell me something they are a fan of, and I'll work off of that.

By chatting with them and not just starting the shoot cold, they feel more at ease, which usually produces a better photo.

All of this rapport building, in my opinion, is the most important aspect of the photoshoot. And it all happens within the usual 15-minute timeframe I have with them.

I treat everyone equally, whether they are the 60-year-old CEO or the newly hired 21-year-old. I tell the same stupid jokes and comments.

But it's important to read people. While some are OK with you, every once in a while, you get some people that are really shut down and have no interest in opening up. Do your best, but don't make them feel more uncomfortable.

Do your best to use their name throughout the shoot. Is shows you are paying attention to them and that they are a unique person and not just another warm body in front of you.

I also feel comfortable enough to tell people when they look bad without making them feel bad. I'll say, "If you are going for the ax murderer look, then you are doing a great job." Even though it sounds like an "insult", they know I'm joking and often smile where I get a great shot. So, make sure you get a few shots right after you say something that may be shocking or funny.

Chapter 10: Posing the Subject

Shoulders at an Angle

First, I have them stand on a line of tape that I have on the floor. I place it so they will be facing my main KEY light. I'll tell them, "put your toes on the tape." Keeping your body in the same direction as the light, just turn your face towards me." You'll be surprised at how difficult this will be for some people. Or you can find an object in the room and tell the subject to stand facing the "X", and then turn your head towards me.

This is classic in most portraiture. Look at any painting, and you will almost never see someone sitting or standing with their chests pointed directly at the artist. To me, square-on shoulders, make the photo look like a mug shot.

The more of an extreme angle, the more "regal" or "stuffy" photo tends to look. I tend not to shoot like this unless that's the feel a client wants or if I feel it will suit them. They will have to twist their face hard to the camera and it isn't always comfortable. Also, the heavier the person is, the worse the chin and neckline will look if they have to twist a lot.

I usually position the shoulders at a 30-45-degree angle from me. I usually have the left shoulder be forward shoulder and set up the lights accordingly. Statistically they say the left side of the face is the better.

I will then tell them to remember that rope and exaggerate the tall posture.

It's for this reason that I like my subject to be standing. Clothes and jackets also flow better and don't bunch up as they might if they are sitting.

Also, I want their shoulders to be even height or have the rear shoulder dip down slightly. If you look at a one-dollar bill, you will see George Washington with his right shoulder forward and his rear left shoulder slightly lower.

Head Tilt

It's important the head never tilt in the opposite direction of the chest. In general, the top of the head should be straight or very slightly tilted in the direction of the chest or far/rear shoulder. It has the effect of "weakening" the subject, if the top of the head is tilted towards the forward shoulder.

Double Chin

It seems everyone complains about having a double chin. To help with this you can have your subject bring their nose forward towards the camera without leaning the upper body forward. This will stretch the skin under the chin. You may want them to bring their chin down as well. This is harder to do with a strong shoulder angle, so you may want to adjust your subject.

Smile vs No Smile

I always ask my clients if they want to smile and look approachable in their photos. Most will and that is certainly my style, even for serious lawyers. And the management who are hiring you will usually want the company employees to be portrayed as friendly approachable people. I always recommend that you also do some no teeth shots. I try and convince my subjects to still have warm welcoming eyes, but without the big smile. You don't want them to look like an intimidating ax murderer, so you need to let your subjects know if they are too serious.

Also keep in mind that the smile can be too big and therefore, not professional and business like. Don't smile like you just won the lottery. In general, I like teeth to show, but no lower teeth if possible and also no space below the front teeth. Some people can't smile like this, so you have to coach them to do their best. But it needs to look natural.

Be aware of the tongue pushers; they will push their tongue out while they smile. It doesn't look good and really hard to retouch out.

If you are having a hard time during the shoot, I will stop and show them the photos and tell them what I would like them to change if they can. People are very often not aware of how their expression looks. By having your camera tethered to the computer, you can give them instant feedback. It's a little easier than showing them the small screen on the camera.

When your client is starting to give you a fake forced smile, I will call them out on it and say, "That is the fakest smile ever!" Be prepared to take a shot right away because nine times out of ten, they will smile, and you will have a great shot. I'll then say, "I just insulted you and you smiled." Be prepared to get another great shot! Every once in a while, I have to tell the client I was kidding as they don't smile after. It's a slightly risky move, but it works almost all of the time.

Remember to really know what your client wants. I'm not a big fan of the tough, confident look that some headshot photographers like, so I don't coax that out of my clients. But if I know in advance that's what they want, I will do so. You will develop your own preferences and style, but always remember your client. Better yet, shoot both and sell them more than one image!

Camera Height

When you look at your client's photo, they should appear the same height as you. They shouldn't look shorter or taller. This creates a connection between the viewer of the photo and the subject. They are on equal footing. Your camera will basically need to be centered on their lower lip or slightly lower to achieve this.

You can experiment being above or below your subject. Having the subject look down onto the camera slightly (lower camera height), will give the subject a feeling of power.

Flow of the Shoot

I'll take a few shots and then change their position slightly. As I told them before the shoot, I will guide them on how to pose. I'll use my hand to move my own head, so they know what I want. They just need to mirror me. I may ask for them to move their chin up or down, give me more turtle, or spin their chest to change the shoulder position.

If things feel really awkward, I'll have them switch the direction of how they are standing. If they are initially standing at let's say 40 degrees to the right, I'll have them spin so they are standing 40 degrees to the left. When they are looking at the camera, instead of their left shoulder and left foot forward, they will reverse in the same spot, so their right shoulder and right foot are forward.

Chapter 11: Common Subject Problems

There are many things that can be out of place and ruin a photo. Before you start, do your best to fix everything. While this is a debatable topic, I have no problem touching my clients. I feel it is necessary to do the job properly. Of course, I am professional and make sure my clients feel comfortable. I'll always say, there are a few things I'd like to poke and prod, is it OK if I touch your clothes? No one has ever said no. Naturally, I'm not going to touch a woman's chest area. Most people will appreciate the attention to detail and often tell me so.

(With Covid, I go through this process, but have them fix the issues themselves.)

I start looking from top to bottom.

Hair

Make sure it's neat as possible. I have a mirror and clean comb always. You don't want hair to fall in your subjects' eyes. You want the eyes to be fully viewable. Also, I have women with long hair first bring it all to the back and then have them part it in the middle with each hand behind their head and then have them bring it straight down over their lapels. This gets rid of hair on the shoulders as well as hair on their necks. I always make a joke and say hairy necks went out in the 70's.

Sometimes long hair will get stuck under their collars. The above technique of bringing it behind, makes it easier.

The small stray hairs you can retouch afterwards.

Most of the time, long hair looks best when it is forward. I usually like it on both sides evenly weighted. Make sure one side is not thicker than the other.

But in the end, the client will always decide. I always suggest we do "both" when they are not sure how to wear it. Some put all on one side, some keep it all back, some like and ear showing, others do not. That's where a quick showing of the laptop can help decide which look looks best.

You can also have them put it in a ponytail. This is a lot easier for you as a photographer as hair issues can often take up time. Have some hair bands in your bag.

Also make sure their hair isn't forming a shelf or blinder over their eyes. This will create large shadows that are not appealing and are hard to retouch.

Glasses

Make sure their glasses are clean. I bring a lens cloth for glasses. Make sure that they are tight against the client's nose, so that the top of the glasses don't cross through their eyes. While it may be a pain to deal with, if a client always wears glasses, they should do so in their photos. If it's 50\50, I'll always suggest they take them off or shoot with and without them.

Also make sure they sit straight on the client's face. They may need to bend and adjust them if they are a bit crooked. Don't you do it, let them.

Glasses can also create a diffraction where there appears to be a big dent in a person's face if they are looking at you at an angle. Pay attention to this and move the face so this is eliminated. If there is glare in the glasses, you can ask the client to tilt their glasses down by bringing the arms of the glasses up a bit. Don't do it too much as it may look weird. If they have long hair it is better as they can hide the higher than normal arms of the glasses.

You can also position your lights a bit higher and angle them down more to eliminate the glare.

Lastly, if they must wear glasses and you are having a difficult time getting rid of the glare, I will take a few pictures of them without glasses and swap out the eye portion of the photo. This takes decent retouching skills.

Shirts

If wearing a tie, the shirt's top button should be buttoned. It may often be tight, but if it needs to be buttoned, I will ask them to do so.

If the shirt is too big, the buttoned collar will look sloppy. I have small bag with little accessories, including small A-clamps. I will grab and gather the excess collar material from behind and clip them. I'll say I hope I'm not choking you, but you need to suffer a bit at times to look good. You can also stuff the back of the collar with a folded-up paper towel. This is a big issue and don't overlook it. Many people don't wear proper fitting shirts.

If the collars are floppy for any reason, have fashion tape in your bag. You can get this at a local drug store or on Amazon. It's great to tape down any parts of clothing that don't want to cooperate. Remind the client to remove the tape after the shoot as it may ruin the clothing during washing.

Some shirts have excess material that gets wrinkled near their lapels. I have them pull and tug and tuck the shirt in as tight as they can and may poke and prod a bit more to improve upon it.

Ties

Make sure the knot is tight enough so that you don't see the shirt button. It should be straight.

Make sure the tail of the tie does not poke out of the sides. Make sure they like their knot. Note how much shirt is appearing on either side of the tie. You may need to adjust the tie or pull a jacket lapel over a bit to even it all out.

Camisole

If your client is wearing a camisole under their blazer, sometimes the top edge of the camisole may fall below where you will crop the photo. It will look like they are wearing a blazer with nothing underneath. I'll suggest to them that they pull the front up while pulling the back down to raise the edge, so you get it in the shot.

Sleeveless Dresses

In general, I am not a fan of skin showing anywhere in a headshot. Most of the time, the client will bring a sweater or jacket with them when they are wearing a sleeveless top. They will ask what my preference is. While my standard answer is usually, "let's try both," it is just easier to cover up. There is less distraction that way and it will appear more professional. Now if the person happens to be really jacked, they may want to show their arms off.

Jewelry

My motto is less is more. It can be distracting.
Earrings: Make sure that both earrings show.
Necklaces: Make sure a necklace is sitting evenly on the neck. Also be aware of where the photo will crop. They may want to tighten up a longer necklace or remove it completely.

No Jacket

Sadly, this is a trend as office clothing is more casual these days. People always look like a hot wrinkled mess without a jacket. I always advise men wear jackets. If the client wants this shot, have them remind subjects to bring in a fresh pressed shirt on a hanger and change right before the shoot.

Missing Clothing

If there is a dress code for the shoot, and someone is not dressed properly, I will ask them if they can borrow the missing jacket or tie from someone. If not, I will call the contact person and mention it to them. "Should I shoot them as is or would you like to reschedule this person for another day?" You can pack a solid gray tie as a loaner if you want.

Lint

"Oh, so you decided to sleep in you suit, cuddled up with you dog last night I see." No, I have never said that, but I've thought it many times. Some people, no matter how professional, can be hot messes. Bring a lint roller or have them wrap tape, sticky side out around their hand and get the mess off. "You can just retouch it" shouldn't be the first choice. It takes time, effort and money.

Shine

Do a test shot to see how shiny your subject is. I always carry small "Oil Absorption Sheets" which you can buy at most drug stores. They are miracle workers. While performers and actors may use makeup artists, most corporate clients do not. The timing just doesn't allow for it or budget constraints prevent it. Some photographers require makeup artists, but for me, I'd rather not have to deal with the extra variable.

Tiny Eyes

During the shoot, your subjects' eyes may disappear when they smile. The bigger the smile, the smaller the eyes. This is natural. If they get too small, I sometimes suggest that they raise their eyelashes as little as they possibly can. Very often this will make them look crazy and not natural. You have to experiment a bit. My style is big smiles. In these rare cases, I will have them tone down the smile.

Many people have one eye that is smaller than the other. You can rotate their head so that the tiny eye is directly at the camera and the bigger eye is slightly turned back and away from the camera. If you have the skill, this can also be fixed in Photoshop with the liquify tool. You can also ask them to try and open the small eye or close down the big eye, knowing it's not that easy to do.

Teeth

Have them check their smile to make sure breakfast isn't stuck in their teeth. Ask them to throw out any gum if they are chewing it.

Eyebrows

Hopefully they are groomed before you show up. Some men can have overgrown eyebrows that are all over the place. I'll ask the client to try and tame them as best they can.

Fresh Haircut

If someone makes the mistake of getting a haircut the hour before a photoshoot, they will have a face and shirt full of tiny hairs. If you notice, ask them to go into the bathroom and clean up as best they can.

Chapter 12: Reviewing the Shoot

As I stated in the beginning, every photographer has their own way of doing things. For me, I want the client to pick their photo right away.

As I shoot tethered, I like to use the Adobe Lightroom Classic™ XY view to pick the favorite photo. I may narrow down the selections by flagging their favorites.

When they pick their favorite for retouching, I will give it 5 stars in Lightroom™. Better yet, I'll go to the folder where the file exists and change the filename to include their full name.

I name my files: Lastname_Firstname_filenumber.jpg. This way I know for sure what file(s) I am to send to the retoucher.

Another method is to upload the images online for the client to pick. It's really important to have your filenames clearly identified. I have had clients send me back the image they want attached in an email in a way I can't determine what file it is. Never try and guess. I've retouched images and then they have said, it was the wrong one. You will not work on the one you send them as they are only proof size.

I upload the files to my website where they can view the proofs. They will be smaller files. But sometimes they take forever to decide. This upload method is good when you don't have a lot of time to shoot many people.

Chapter 13: Retouch & Delivery

The best advice I can give you if you want to take this seriously as a business (and not as an art or a hobby), is to outsource your retouching. For some photographers, this is sacrilege; I think that's nonsense. If you do your own retouching, you will certainly have more control over your final product, but you will also spend hours and hours doing this work.

Seriously listen to me! Find three retouchers that you like that have reasonable prices. I have stubbornly fought this for years. I'd find a retoucher, they would do a good job for a few images and then start to suck. I'd then just do my own retouching and then start the process of finding a new one a year later. The same thing would happen over and over again. I would always say they all sucked. But this isn't how business works. Henry Ford certainly didn't build cars by himself and he certainly wasn't welding.

I now have an amazing retoucher. I have so much free time, it's silly. In the past I would spend hours a day retouching. Now I do none. Try Upwork.com, Fiverr.com, Google, Facebook Groups, etc., and send out a photo to a ton of retouchers. Review their work.

Always have one or two backup retouchers ready as your favorite may quit or disappoint you. Spend an hour a week looking for new retouchers. I have found someone that specializes in beauty retouching. That means they only work on skin and faces. You will find a lot of foreign companies that do all types, product, clothing, etc. I don't want them. I want to work with one individual and not be passed around to different people within a company. As of 2020, I wouldn't spend more than $20 per image on a retoucher. I currently spend $12 per image. In the event I don't like part of a retouch, rather than send it back, I'll fix it myself. For this reason, I never have the retoucher crop the images. That way I can layer the original image under the retouched and mask out and change the small detail I want fixed. This way I can also see what they worked on by layering the retouched and unretouched images. Clients may also want different crops so it's always best to crop yourself.

Whoever does the retouching, just make sure it looks natural and not fake and plastic. No one wants fake and plastic. Some retouchers, especially beauty retouchers, love perfect flawless skin which is never realistic.

File Delivery

I'll make note of what size my client wants to receive the photos in. If they don't have a specific requirement, I'll crop to 8"x10" at 300ppi. This a large file around 2-3 megabytes that they can always make smaller.

I'll rename the file to include the 8x10, so Last_First_8x10_file number.jpg

If it's a few files, I'll either send multiple emails with 6 attached files each or use a webservice like WeTransfer.com or Dropbox.com

Most emails cannot handle more than 20MB of attachments.

You can also use your website to deliver the images if it has the capabilities. Zenfolio.com has galleries for clients to download images.

Chapter 14: Your Company Details

Company Name

The easiest way to name your business is to call it "Your Name Photography".

Business Structure

As I wrote this book for a complete beginner, I wouldn't jump into starting a corporation right away. You may find that it isn't for you in the long run.

In the USA, you can fill out a DBA, Doing Business As form to create a Sole Proprietorship. This does not provide the legal and tax benefits that a corporation provides. Look into a LLC or and S-Corporation. Talk to an accountant or lawyer about this.

Banking

Open up a separate checking account to run your expenses through. You do not want to mix your personal finances with your businesses.

Credit Card for Expenses

Apply for a business credit card to pay for all of your expenses. If you can't get one for any reason, then just use a separate credit card and only use it for business expenses. Again, do not mix your personal and business expenses.

Square or PayPal Business Account

You need to be able to accept credit cards. A Square or PayPal account is the easiest way to accept credit cards. I have a PayPal business account that I started many years ago. I can swipe credit cards on my iPhone, and they gave me a debit card that I can make purchases or withdraw cash from an ATM. Naturally I can transfer the money into my business checking account.

There are also apps like Venmo or Zelle where you can accept payment. Find an option that is easy for your clients.

Chapter 15: Website & Domain Names

You must have a website to display your photography and to explain your services offered. There are many solutions to choose from. I suggest you use a website platform that is premade for photographers. It will just make things easier for you and you should be able to make all the changes by yourself without having to hire a web developer.

Zenfolio.com is a highly recommended platform to display your portfolio. In addition, you can offer proofing and scheduling. This will run approximately $30 per month.

Format.com is another platform that is great for photographers that will run between $18-$25 a month.

Squarespace.com has themes that are made for displaying photos.

Wix.com is cheaper alternative.

You could also use **WordPress.org**. While it is popular, it's not the easiest to edit if you wish to build it yourself.

Scheduling

Your website platform may have this built in, but if it doesn't there are third party platforms that you may be able to use.

I added the free version of **Acuity** Scheduling to my WordPress website and within days, I was notified of a scheduled photoshoot. It felt like free money coming from the sky. Naturally I had to do the work, but it was nice, no phone calls, no emails, no questions. Just a notification that a person has booked a shoot.

But my website also contains a lot of information, including prices.

Calendly is another service like Acuity Scheduling. New products may also be available for you to research.

Domain Name

As your company may be called Your Name Photography, your domain name should be close as well. I would always use a .com address and not include hyphens.

Ideas include:

Yourname.com
YouNamePhotography.com
YourNamePhoto.com
YourNameHeadshots.com
YourNamePortraits.com
YourNameHeadshotsCity.com

Use a website like InstantDomainSearch.com to check to see if your domain is available.

Email Address

It's best if you can use your domain name rather than Gmail.com. It may cost $10\month, but it will look professional. Don't use your old personal email.

Chapter 16: Your Portfolio

Your portfolio is going to be on your website.

It is important that it focuses on what your clients want. I shoot corporate headshots and my website only displays corporate headshots. I personally believe that you should only have one genre of photography on your website and would use multiple websites for different genres.

As I said everyone does things differently. I think the money and extra effort is worth it marketing wise, to look like a specialist and not a generalist.

If you needed knee surgery and one doctor says they can do all types of surgery and the other says they only specialize in knee surgery, I would think you would be more likely to feel confident with the specialist.

What to Include

You should only have your best images of well-dressed professionals on your website.

It is ALWAYS better to have less images that are high quality vs a lot of images with low quality. If you are promoting corporate headshots, make sure you only have corporate headshots. While I did state you should be a specialist, I do think it's OK to mix performer headshots on your website, but in a different section. Don't put a teenage actor wearing a t-shirt in your corporate headshot section.

Do whatever it takes to get 20 images. Offer real estate agents free photos provided they dress professionally. Do the same with an insurance agency or any company. Just start contacting anyone and everyone.

If you belong to a house of worship, offer to photograph the main staff. Religious garments may be a distraction so keep the clothing professional.

You should have a mix of people in your portfolio, so all are represented. People want to see themselves in the photos you take. While it's nice to have pretty people on your website, have a mixture of all types.

Use a few different backgrounds so it doesn't look like your entire portfolio came from one shoot. Don't have one subject that wears different clothes in different locations. I see that a lot with beginners.

Chapter 17: The Answer is Yes!

One of the reasons for my success is that my answer to all of my client requests is yes. I am not a Prima donna.

Can you come now? Yes

Can you send the retouched images the same day of the shoot? Yes

There is a long-time gap between people, is that OK? Yes

Can you send a bill and well pay in 30 days? Yes

Can you shoot in this teeny tiny room? Yes

Can you come to this far off location? Yes

Can you come for one person? Yes

Almost all requests are free, I don't nickel and dime my clients, except for long distance travel. Now I'm not a push over. If the client is asking for something really out of line, I will charge extra for it. But it's more important for me to have the reputation of being easy and fun to work with. I make my money because I keep getting called back by my clients multiple times a year.

Chapter 18: Marketing

Branding Basics

Every communication and interaction a client has with your business should create a specific impression. This also includes your own appearance and how you dress.

I bet if you went to a fictious "Frank's Used Autos" the entire experience would be different than if you went to a Rolls-Royce dealership.

Work on having a consistent, polished message.

Social Media

You should create a separate business account for the dominant social media platforms and post once a week. You can post the same content to all of them or just make slight changes.

Pick a specific day and make it a routine. You can post tips, samples of your photoshoot, behind the scenes images and special offers. Every once in a while, you can post something personal about you, but don't do it too often. It adds a human touch, but don't confuse these accounts with your own personal accounts.

I would start with LinkedIn, Instagram and Facebook. But who knows what will be the next best thing. Just keep up with it.

Honestly, I never use social media for my business. I know it's a mistake and it is something I would recommend everyone use. I am sure if I spent the time on it, my business would double.

Google My Business

One of the best things you can do is get a Google My Business listing. After you are verified, you will be displayed on Google maps and come up in local searches.

Reviews

One of the most important things you can do is ask for reviews from you clients. This is considered social proof, and this will defiantly generate more business for you. The reviews can be placed on your Google Business Listing. You can also copy theses reviews on to a Testimonials page on your website.

Google Advertising

This is certainly tricky as you can sometimes spend a lot of money on ads and not get business. The platform can be quite overwhelming, but Google has its own staff to help you. You can schedule an appointment for a Google representative to call you and they will help you. There is no charge or fee for this extra help. Don't confuse this with the random calls you will get from people pretending to work for Google and they are just independent advertising agencies that will setup your Google ads for a fee.

Other Advertising Platforms

Some people have luck with other platforms. Yelp and Thumbtack are two that come to mind. They are more for individuals who are looking for your service at a low price. But it may work for you to get started.

LinkedIn Ads

You can advertise on LinkedIn and you can also get leads emailed to you from people looking for headshots with their "**ProFinder**" program. I would experiment and see if this can work out for you and your business.

Email System

Open up a **MailChimp.com** account and start gathering your clients email addresses. You should send out a message to your clients every 2-3 months, so you are fresh in their minds. Don't always be spammy and try for sales. Maybe take interesting pictures of your area's landmarks that they would enjoy seeing. Just make sure they are really nice images. Don't send out crappy photos and ruin your reputation.

Zenfolio.com also offers this type of email system for capturing emails and sending out info regularly to your clients.

Generating More Business

Besides everything mentioned in this book, make a list of every company in your area that you want to do business with. Find a CRM system that works best for you and start to add the details to these companies. You usually want to contact the Marketing Manager. Hubspot.com has a free starter account you can try.

Reach out every 4 months in some capacity. If it's a call, just say, "I know you have a photographer but if you ever need to add a backup, I'm available and can offer you X.

Do you have any needs now, where we can do a trial?"

This is one of the hard parts of running your business, but it is a necessary evil. The more you do this, the faster you will make more money. Also think long term. What is the lifetime value of one new client? If you get one client a week, what will that mean for you in 3 years?

Search Local Companies Websites

You can find new clients by looking at company websites and search for missing photos on the headshot page.

Contact the individual or if you can find a marketing person, reach out to them and give them a great offer.

Contact Local Photographers

Many photographers specialize in certain areas and turn down work that they are not comfortable with. Reach out to all of your local photographers and work out a deal for any referrals they can give you.

Referral Fees

ALWAYS pay people that refer you business! I can't stress this enough. I am not referring to company managers where it's their job to hire you (although you can make that argument), but those who are doing it to be nice and of service. A $20, a $50, or even a free photo session will be remembered.

Business Cards

Hand out your business card to every individual that you photograph at companies. Even though they are not your end customer as the company is paying for it, they may contact you for future photos. I often get calls from spouses saying you took my wife's\husband's photo and I need one. As a perfect example, I got a text recently from a guy I photographed a year ago. He wants a quick outdoor portrait of his son which I will be shooting in a few days as I write this.

You can also ask them if they want to be on your personal mailing list and open your phone to your mailing list opt-in for individuals.

Chapter 19: Invoicing

There are many ways you can send invoices to your clients. PayPal has a built-in invoice feature as does Square. You can also use a service like 17Hats.com.

Zenfolio.com has invoicing built into its service as well.

Or you can simply create a Google Document or MS Word Document and type in the info each time you do a shoot.

Your Company Photography
Company Address, City, State Zip Code
Phone: 555-555-5555
Tax ID: 55-5555 555
www.Yourwebsite.com
email@email.com

INVOICE

INVOICE #:

DATE:

TOTAL DUE: $

TO:

Client Company Name
Client Company Address
Contact Name

　　Please remit $ for photo shoot on Month x, year for headshots.

Payment due upon receipt.
Make checks payable to: Your Company Online:
http://www.yourwebsite/payments

Chapter 20: Pricing

You can NOT be the cheap option in your market. It is really hard, especially for a beginner to hear and comprehend this idea. They figure since they are new, the easiest way to compete is on price. IT IS A MISTAKE! You will work yourself ragged just to get by. Banking on volume just isn't a good idea.

With a low price, you will also be perceived as a low-quality option. You want to build your brand to be like the Rolls-Royce ™ or Tiffany ™ of headshots. Do not be Joe's Bargain Basement Headshots. Be in the top 1/3rd of pricing at the very least.

Always Have an Upsell

There are many things that a client will want. While they may call for "just a headshot", they may need serious and casual, different looks, different hair styles, different backgrounds, added digital backgrounds, different locations. You may offer them prints, B&W versions, different digital sizing. Some clients want all the images for a flat fee. You can easily modify the background with different colored gels.

Consider a base price or session fee plus a fee for each delivered\retouched photo. Make it easy for clients to buy multiple photos. If you can allow the time during your shoot to make the above listed variations.

"Let's try something different" is the line I use to change things up. This won't always work with companies but may be easier with individuals.

You can also offer some super artistic retouching to their final image for an additional fee. If you go to https://www.youtube.com/c/bluelightningtv/ they have tutorials on how to turn photos into currency, cartoons, pop art, and other highly artistic, stylized images. Make a printed sample booklet of a regular headshot and then all of the "treatments" you can add for an additional fee. Even if you have a company paying for the standard headshot, you can upsell the individuals on these alternative images. You may want to ask the manager who hired you first if it is OK to promote this upsell to the employees. You could make a free sample for that person, so they get on board with the idea.

No Minimums

I will go to a client even for one person. While other competitors may have minimums, I don't and it's a way to get new clients. I charge extra for one person as that covers my setup and travel fee.

My Rates

For Manhattan, my rates are on the reasonable side. But because I'm usually shooting multiple people for each visit, I'm happy with the money I generate.

I charge $250 for the first person and then $150 for each additional person. This price includes retouching of 1 photo each. I charge $50 if someone wants a second photo retouched. I like simple and this works for me and my clients.

I take 30 minutes to setup my lighting and then each person gets 15 minutes. It takes about 15 minutes to pack up and I'm on to my next shoot. A typical 4-person shoot takes me under 2 hours, and I bill $700. My retoucher costs me $48. I often see 2 clients per day, and I'm usually working 5 days a week.

I also walk to most of my clients because I despise commuting. For most of my working life I have always lived walking distance to work. That will never change.

Chapter 21: Miscellaneous Best Business Practices

Strike while the iron is hot. When you get an inquiry, respond immediately. Wait a day and they job will go to someone else. Wait even an hour and you may lose.

Create a written agreement or contract between you and your client. Know what they want and deliver it.

Collect a payment to secure your shoot. This will weed out the non-serious people.

Larger corporations may want to be billed. I always agree and never had a problem collecting payment. I actually like having a large accounts receivable balance as I know there will be money coming in. But stay on top of the late payers. So many times, my invoices have slipped through the cracks and I needed to send out reminder emails. But it's usually the same clients. A billion-dollar financial organization comes to mind. They still owe me $600 from 5 months ago! I'm not worried, they will pay, they always do. I won't huff and puff as it is not my contacts fault. They appreciate my patience. I know the drill.

Be flexible and say yes as often as you can. Don't be petty.

Always try an offer an upsell. Additional shots, additional time, multiple looks, different backgrounds, different file formats.

Reshoot if client is not happy. Every once in a while, I will review the photos with a client, and they aren't happy. I'll always ask specifically what they don't like. Even taking just an extra 5-10 shots often works wonders and turns an unhappy client into a happy one. But I always ask, what don't you like? Get specifics. That extra round of photos that literally takes under 2 minutes makes all the difference.

Keep in mind that some people you will just never be able to please. After finishing a shoot with a balding 50+ year old attorney, he told me he hated the photos and then proceeded to show me his college ID photo showing a full thick head of black hair from 30 years ago!

He wanted to look like this. I told him he needed therapy and to pick the photo he hates the least.

Stay patient and keep smiling. Some people will try your nerves. They will all appreciate you working with them and staying patient.

Backup your files! Write to multiple cards if your camera can.

Chapter 22: Final Thoughts

You will never stop learning as a photographer. I encourage you to experiment with different lighting setups and backgrounds and always get feedback from your clients. Every so often, I'll say to my subject, "So I'm done shooting you. I know I have a lot of good shots for you to choose from, but if you have a few minutes, I wouldn't mind giving you some bonus shots. It will only take a few minutes." Most people will be happy to oblige. I then will experiment with a new lighting setup.

Also, look at other photographer's work. See what you like about it. Analyze the light.

Take classes and workshops. Get together with other photographers, socialize and share.

Post your photos and ask for constructive criticism. You may find that you don't see the things that other photographers see. I once was watching a photographer critique another photographer's photo and they said they didn't like the shadow that was on the collar of the shirt. I didn't notice it. It bothered me that I didn't see it. So, it's good to get other eyes involved. They will help you to see more. And as a good photographer, that's what you are constantly doing, scanning for things that don't look right. Strive for perfection.

If you like the way I write, I also published on Amazon:

The Art of War for Photographers: The Mindset Needed for a Successful Photography Business – It focuses on the mental game needed for success, taken from the basic principles of the original Art of War.

Lastly, checkout https://shootforthemoney.com/headshot-book for more tips, ideas and updates.

I wish you all the success that you deserve.

Chapter 23: Resources

These websites are recommended for you to use to build your photography business.

Photography Training - https://shootforthemoney.com/headshot-book

Photography Equipment - Bhphotovideo.com

Photography Equipment - Amazon.com

Domain Names - NameCheap.com

Portfolio Website - Zenfolio.com

Software - Adobe.com

Business Cards - Moo.com

Email Marketing - Mailchimp.com

Invoicing - 17Hats.com

Tether Equipment - Tethertools.com

File Transfer - WeTransfer.com

www.ingramcontent.com/pod-product-compliance
Lightning Source LLC
Chambersburg PA
CBHW071121240526
45465CB00022B/757